IMAGES OF ALSACE

DELLA MEYERS & KIERA TCHELISTCHEFF

PHOTOGRAPHY BY
FRÉDÉRIC ENGEL
AND GENEVIÈVE ENGEL

PHOTOGRAPHS

FRÉDÉRIC ENGEL: & **GENEVIÈVE ENGEL**

ISBN 2-9524377-0-X

EAN-9782952437707

FIRST PUBLISHED IN FRANCE IN 2005 BY
THE BOOKWORM
3 RUE DE PÂQUES
67000 STRASBOURG
PHONE: +33 (0) 3 88 32 26 99
WWW.BOOKWORM.FR

DÉPÔT LÉGAL SEPTEMBRE 2005

© TOUS DROITS RÉSERVÉS

TEXT © DELLA MEYERS & KIERA TCHELISTCHEFF
DESIGN AND LAYOUT © THE BOOKWORM 2005
PHOTOGRAPHS © FRÉDÉRIC ENGEL & GENEVIÈVE ENGEL
ILLUSTRATIONS © PAT THIÉBAUT
WALLPAPERS © MUSÉE DU PAPIER PEINT, RIXHEIM

COPY EDITOR: JOSIANE WOODS
DESIGN AND LAYOUT: C. WEHRLE FOR: WWW.T-L-P.COM
RECIPES: GABY OSTERMANN

"You don't know how it has happened but it appears that you have grown older... and now consider it the right time to visit ALSACE"

Véronique Schnell Feugeas

Acknowledgements

WE WOULD LIKE TO EXPRESS OUR MOST PROFOUND GRATITUDE TO THE FOLLOWING FOR THEIR CONTRIBUTIONS TO OUR BOOK :

Vincent Froehlicher for believing in the project from the start;
Maryvonne Génaux-Vonach also known as "Mao";
Louise Meyers for her unfailing support over a lifetime;
Gaby Ostermann who provided all the mouth-watering recipes;
Josiane Woods for her care and expertise, Lilly Pharmaceuticals
and our most heartfelt thanks to Pat Thiébaut for his wonderful illustrations.

« QUEL BEAU JARDIN ! »

« WHAT A BEAUTIFUL GARDEN » EXCLAIMED LOUIS XIV UPON VIEWING
THE LUSH PANORAMA OF ALSACE FOR THE FIRST TIME. WITH ITS ROLLING
VINEYARDS, IMPOSING CASTLES AND PICTURESQUE VILLAGES, ALSACE IS
TRULY A TREAT TO BEHOLD!

*T*hrough our selection of images we hope to inspire those who have yet to explore the riches of the region, to come and discover an endearing people and their fascinating history. Faceted by contradictions resulting from painful and turbulent events, Alsatians retain a strong sense of cultural identity, often misunderstood. Having changed nationalities four times in a period of 75 years between 1870 and 1945 when they were used as a pawn between France and Germany, they feel profoundly French and European today.

Although attached to their traditions, their dynamism and sense of innovation attract many foreign investors. Combining serious work ethics with a certain joie de vivre, sceptical by nature yet open-minded, they also have the ability to make fun of themselves. The Alsatian language is still widely spoken by the older generation and understood by the young who enjoy a great moment of mirth during their traditional bilingual socio-political satires.

Taste the flavour of *Er het Hoor uf de Zähn!*: "He has hair on his teeth" which is to say that he is a nasty character to realize what a colourful mode of expression Alsatian can be!

The aspects we have chosen to present in this volume stem from our personal tastes and experiences after years of living in Alsace. Our aim is to share that which has been so much a part of our lives, and we hope that our enthusiasm and attachment to this region will be reflected in the pages to come.

Della & Kiera

CONTENTS

ᴀRCHITECTURAL HERITAGE

The architecture of Alsace is one of the most distinctive in France and is as rich as its cultural and culinary heritage. The well-kept towns of today still reflect the flourishing past with their superb homes, town halls and squares.

The topography of the typical Alsatian village has changed little since its conception: tidy rows of half-timbered farmhouses continue to line the main street in close proximity to the village church.

Fine examples of religious architecture can be seen throughout the region, spanning several centuries, from the Romanesque to the Baroque. A visit to Alsace would not be complete without exploring one of the numerous castles perched on top of the verdant hills.

*Medieval town of **Kaysersberg**, originally called in Roman times Caesaris Mons, the Emperor's Mountain. It was developed by subsequent emperors because of its strategic position.*

CIVIL ARCHITECTURE

It is not uncommon for first-time visitors to the region to be struck by the similarities with German culture and architecture. Indeed, Alsace has retained much of its Germanic heritage, having been a part of the Holy Roman Empire for over eight centuries starting at the beginning of the ninth century under Charlemagne.

Petite France, Strasbourg. *The timber-framed corbelled houses date back to the 16th and 17th centuries, formerly home to the fishermen's, tanners' and millers' guilds.*

Thanks to the riches of the convents and monasteries, Alsace was already at that time a prosperous region, but its period of greatest prosperity began in the twelfth century during the reign of the Hohenstaufen Emperors who favoured the rise of a wealthy merchant class and powerful guilds also known as trade associations. Notwithstanding the vicissitudes of history, such as poor harvests, outbreaks of the bubonic plague, invasions and peasant revolts which tested the population's resistance and resilience, towns and cities continued to thrive throughout the reign of the Habsburgs.

The Thirty Years War 1618-1648 devastated Alsace as troops from as far a field as Spain and Sweden, as well as France and Austria, ravaged the land, pillaging and ransacking villages, which along with famine and disease decimated the populace. The conclusion of the war marked the end of the rule of the Holy Roman Emperors over Alsace and for the first time in its history it became French when it was annexed to France by Louis XIV. Under the French, Alsace once again rebuilt itself into a thriving and prosperous region.

left: **Old Town, Colmar**

Floral balcony in the ancient imperial town of **Turckheim**. *To this day, from May to October, Alsace's last night watchman still roams the streets stopping and singing at every street corner.*

Like their Flemish counterparts, Alsatian towns were governed by powerful town councils whose beautiful Town Halls were the focal points around which the wealthy merchants built their homes. Elaborately decorated half-timbered houses, such as the Maison Kammerzell in Strasbourg or the Maison Katz in Saverne, graced city centres and flaunted their owners' wealth and pride. Many were three-tiered buildings with gabled roofs, often adorned with an oriel window which not only made the house visible from afar but also allowed the occupant to watch the street's hustle and bustle, unnoticed.

The imprint left by eight centuries of prosperity under German rule can still be admired today in most Alsatian towns such as Colmar, Saverne, Wissembourg, Sélestat, Obernai, Riquewihr and Ribeauvillé, to name but a few.

Westercamp Museum, Wissembourg. Built in 1599, it was the home of a local wine grower. It now carries the name of a prominent notary who donated it to the city of Wissembourg. The museum retraces local history and folklore.

«Fontaine de la Licorne» Fountain of the Unicorn, in Saverne's town centre.

The Dolder, Riquewihr. The former belfry erected in 1291 now houses a local museum. Untouched by the two world wars, this prosperous historical village is one of the most well preserved examples of Alsatian architecture along the Route des Vins.

Remarkable roof of the *Maison du Sel, Wissembourg.* Built in 1448, it was the first hospital in the city. It was turned into a salt warehouse before becoming a slaughterhouse in the 17th century.

Maison Katz, Saverne.
Built in 1605 for Henri Katz, the tax collector for the bishopric. Beautifully preserved home, noted for its richly sculpted façade and angled oriel window

RURAL ARCHITECTURE

Half-timbered houses exist in other regions in France but are particularly characteristic of the Alsatian village. Their form and function often vary from one village to the next but certain characteristics are common to all rural homes.

*A view of the charming village of **Boersch**. First mentioned in the local history of the region in the early 12th century*

*left: Typical half-timbered 16th century house in **Turckheim***

*windows: **Ecomusée** d'Alsace*

*right: Village of **Bergheim**, once the property of the Habsburg family in the 14th century, later owned by the Birkenfeld family until the French Revolution.*
It was the only village to offer the right of asylum as all churches would offer the right of sanctuary.

Sometimes, the farmhouse is large enough to have the living area, the barn and the stables under one roof, such as in the Sundgau region in the south. At others, the owner's home is separate from the barn and stables such as in the Kochersberg area further north. A prominent feature of wealthier farmhouses is the entrance gate which is in fact composed of two arched doorways, a small one to allow entry for the owners and their guests, and a much larger one for the animal-drawn hay-filled carts. The layout of the typical Alsatian village is most often one farmhouse next to another linked by adjoining walls, facing one another on either side of the main street. Although villages have grown tremendously over the years with city dwellers in search of another way of life, the initial design has remained more or less intact.

*House of **Koetzingue**, the first house to be transferred to the site of the future **Ecomuseum** in 1980. A typical house where the poorest families lived squeezed into two rooms with a minuscule kitchen.*

*Village of **Rodern**. First mentioned in official documents dating back to 814.*

The gates are usually closed and one cannot begin to imagine the wealth of the farmers living within.

The Alsatians are proud of their homes and one can often see lovely floral arrangements on the balconies of the windows. In contrast to modern-day houses, constructions such as these let in little light, with small windows and low ceilings. Nevertheless, they are still much sought-after as part of the local heritage as well as a sound investment and it is not rare to see houses painted in vivid hues dotting the landscape.

The Ecomusée in the little village of Ungersheim south of Colmar is a life-size museum of the different farmhouses. All of the houses were transplanted from various villages throughout Alsace to the museum whose aim is to preserve the architectural and cultural heritage of the area. While these were indeed moved in order to save them from total destruction, it was common for houses in general to be transferred from one place to another. An exceptional case occurred in 1776 after the Rhine river flooded and the entire village of Kunheim was displaced, to prevent it from future flood damage.

Houses were made either of stone or half-timbered frames in-filled with wattle and daub. The advantages of the latter were that they were easy and inexpensive to build, resistant and well insulated, in addition to being mobile.

The Wine Producer's house at the Ecomuseum.
Built in 1706, it is typical in that the cellar can be reached directly from the courtyard and an exterior staircase leads to the dwelling area on the second floor.

RELIGIOUS ARCHITECTURE

Typical Romanesque architecture in France spans the 10th, 11th and the early 12th centuries, originating in the 10th with the Cluniac order. Highlights of Romanesque art can be seen in the southwest of France such as the Abbey in Moissac as well as in the Burgundy area; a superb example of late Romanesque architecture being the Abbey of Vezelay.

These were resting spots for weary pilgrims on their way to Santiago de Compostela in Spain. Early Romanesque architecture is characterised by its simplicity: walls are short and squat, allowing for small alabaster-filled windows, letting in very little light. The inside is usually as sober as the outside with little to no decoration. In later Romanesque architecture, the capitals supporting the columns become increasingly imaginative, transporting the viewer into a world of heaven or hell, showing stories from the Old Testament.

Although one does not naturally associate Alsace with Romanesque art, it also has its *Route Romane* or Romanesque Route, with splendid examples throughout the area such as the church of St Peter and St Paul in Rosheim, and the abbey churches of Marmoutier, Murbach and Ottmarsheim, the latter consecrated by the Alsatian Pope Leo IX in 1049. The churches were built in the Germanic style, since Alsace was at the heart of the Holy Roman Empire.

Church of Saint Pierre et Saint Paul, Rosheim. *Built in the 12th century, it is one of the finest examples of Romanesque architecture in Alsace. Distinguishing features are the Lombardian banding on the west front and walls, the use of yellow sandstone and the 16th century octagonal belfry surmounting the crossing. Also includes a restored Silbermann organ of 1733.*

As a consequence the Romanesque age came later to Alsace and lasted much longer than in France where Gothic architecture was already flourishing. The colour and grain of the pink and yellow sandstone, quarried locally, give the exteriors a decorative aspect not commonly seen elsewhere as well as a certain warmth to the interior, mitigating its usual austerity.

The floor plan of most of the churches is a homogeneous T-shape with short transept arms, and the capitals strike the viewer by their simplicity. Lantern towers and belfries are also distinctive features of the Alsatian Romanesque church.

Church of Saint Pierre et Saint Paul, Rosheim.

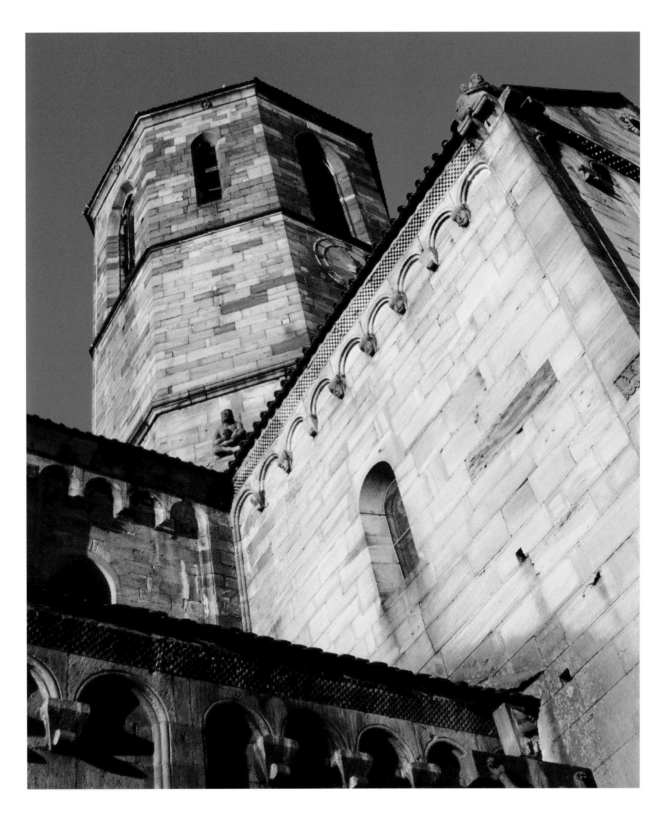

*Romanesque **Abbey Church of Marmoutier**. Its similarities with the Church of Saint Pierre et Saint Paul date it to the beginning of the 12th century. Its history is a complex one of building and rebuilding but the façade as seen today is a superb example of Romanesque architecture while the interior is in the Gothic style.*

The other distinguishing feature is the organ built by André Silbermann in 1710.

Romanesque **Abbey Church of Murbach**, founded in 727. Famous and wealthy from the start, it was known for its remarkable library. As of the 12th century, the abbots were also princes of the Holy Roman Empire and the monks were aristocrats. Its wealth was such that it owned property in more than 200 places and minted its own coins.

*Old Collegiate **Church Saint-Adelphe of Neuwiller-les-Saverne**, mentioned for the first time in 1147. It served two functions: one as a parish church and the other, after 1497, as home to the canons' chapter who were dependent on the nearby Abbey Church of Saint Pierre et Saint Paul when the Abbey was secularised.*

*Beautiful and most unusual tower of the **Church of Chatenois**, dating back to the 12th century. Its role was a defensive one. The rest of the church is 18th century and features within two wooden engravings of the school of Dürer, a mother of pearl inlaid cross brought back from Jerusalem by the Franciscans and the Silbermann organs made in 1765.*

Convent of Saint-Odile. *One of the most important sites in Alsace visited by tourists, pilgrims and locals. Indeed it is home to one of the most famous legends of Alsace.*

The patron saint of Alsace, Odile, was the daughter of the Duke Adalric. Around 700 AD, she founded a nunnery on a mountain and became its first abbess. The legend tells the tale of Odile, born blind and rejected by her father. Sent by her mother to her uncle Saint Erhard, she miraculously recovered her sight. Against her will, her father then decided to marry her off and pursued her through the forest as she tried to escape her fate. It is said that a rock opened up and enfolded her, thereby saving her from her unwanted destiny.

From that rock, a sacred spring shot forth. In the face of such a miracle, her father renounced his project to marry her and built her a convent. As it was believed that Odile was able to cure sick people with the holy water, pilgrims came from near and far to pray and make use of the curative water. To this day it is a foremost place of pilgrimage, particularly among people with eye afflictions. The Chapelle Saint-Odile gives shelter to an 8th century sarcophagus containing the relics of the saint. The Fontaine Saint-Odile is further down the road in the direction of Saint Nabor.

Gothic architecture first appeared in France with the construction of the narthex and western façade, consecrated in 1140, of the basilica of St. Denis, north of Paris.

Abbot Suger's philosophy, derived from the writings of " Dionysius " a theologian who lived in Syria in the 6th century, is essential in understanding this form of architecture.

The Abbot supported the idea that God reflected harmony and radiance on earth that is to say that God was light. Coloured gems adorned the crosses and liturgical vessels, thereby also reflecting divine light. Stained glass windows were the glory of Gothic churches, their importance being not only in the light they brought in but the messages they conveyed.

Old and New Testament stories became visible to the illiterate faithful and were seen as the source of both spiritual and physical illumination.

Abbot Suger was no architect. However, a new technique was developed to put his philosophy into form. While the main support of the Romanesque churches was their hefty, stout pillars inside, the entire support of the Gothic church was transferred to the outside of the edifice.

The structural weight of the church rested upon the strong buttresses supporting the exterior walls, allowing the architects to open up the interior by building very slim soaring pillars. This also enabled them to provide apertures for the superb stained glass windows with which we are all familiar: typical examples of Gothic architecture are Chartres (1145-1170) and of course, Notre Dame in Paris (1163-1250).

Old convent « des Récollets » in Saverne, built in 1303.

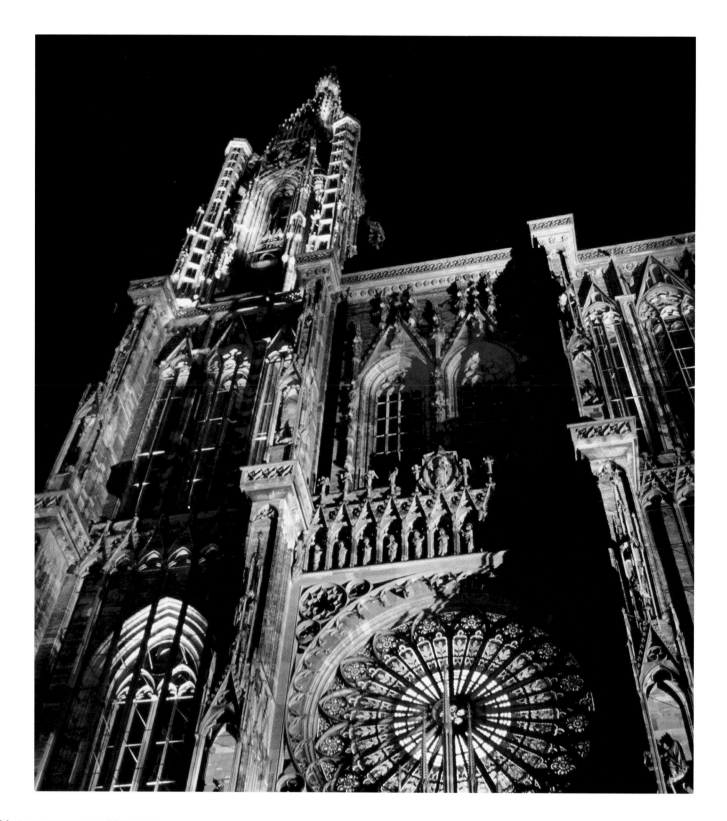

The cathedral of Notre-Dame de Strasbourg is one of the most exquisite examples of Gothic architecture and its beauty is further enhanced by the use of pink sandstone from the Vosges. Work on the cathedral began in 1176 on the site of a previous Romanesque church destroyed by fire in 1145. Its construction spanned many centuries and is a complex one. Strasbourg was termed the city of the roads, and its characteristic single 142m spire, the highest in Europe until the 16th century, symbolized the meeting point of the crossroads of Europe.

Summer illuminations of the **Cathedral of Strasbourg**

Details of the façade of Strasbourg Cathedral.

While discussing religious architecture in Alsace, it seems fitting to present one of the most famous families of organ makers of the 18th century: the Silbermanns.

They were active from 1699 to 1781, beginning with the father André Silbermann who trained his brother Gottfried, as well as his two sons Jean-André and Jean-Daniel. The Silbermanns' legacy in Alsace is the works of André and Jean-André. They turned organ making into an art form in terms of sight, sound and feel. Silbermann organs, all made of oak wood, were designed as well-balanced instruments, visually adapted to the environment for which they were meant, ornate but not overly. They were also notable for their ability to be played in a multitude of tonalities, something which might seem obvious to us today but was certainly novel in the 18th century, and made the Silbermanns' reputation as the foremost craftsmen of their time. Of the 91 organs built by the Silbermanns, many can be visited and heard today, in and around Strasbourg as well as in other towns in Alsace.

Organ built in 1710 from the Church of Saint-Etienne, Marmoutier

TIMOR DOMINI INITIUM SAPIENTIÆ.

Organ built in 1780 from the Protestant Church of Saint-Pierre Le Jeune, Strasbourg

Castle of Birkenfels 13th century.

CHÂTEAUX FORTS

Viewed from the plains or its foothills, the Vosges mountains are dotted with an amazing number of castle ruins: in fact, with some 400 sites, there are more feudal castle ruins in Alsace than in any other region in Europe, not to mention the remains of the medieval fortifications which protected the majority of the villages.

The abundance of châteaux forts can be explained by the power struggles which ensued for control of the Holy Roman Empire and also the riches of the region, natural and mercantile. Despite a number of castles being built during the reign of Charlemagne, castle construction started in earnest in the 12th century when the Hohenstaufens were consolidating their grip on the empire and using Alsace as their base. It was said of Frederick II, Duke of Alsace and brother of Conrad, the Holy Roman Emperor, that « le duc Frédéric traîne toujours après lui, par la queue de son cheval, un château fort », after him, Duke Frederick pulls a castle by the tail of his horse. Conrad's son, Frederick Barbarossa (1122-1190) who became the most powerful of the Holy Roman Emperors, followed in the footsteps of his uncle by adding at least another twenty castles during his reign.

The decline of the Hohenstaufen dynasty lasted through the first half of the 13th century culminating in what was known as the « Grand Interregnum » (1250-1273) when chaos was rampant until the ascendancy of the Habsburgs. Castle construction reached its peak at that time: in theory, permission to build a castle had to be granted by the Emperor. In practice, those who had the means and the temerity to undertake such a costly project did so. These were the emperor's relations and allies, the wealthy families of the nobility competing for power, the knights as well as the increasingly powerful bishops of Strasbourg and Basel.

Kaysersberg Route des Vins

«Mur païen», pagan wall at **Mont St. Odile**

Castle of Haut-Andlau, *built between 1337 and 1344. In a good state of conservation, it is unique in that it features two keeps on either side of the main building. Although the castle was confiscated during the French Revolution, it returned to the Andlau family in the 19th century to whom it still belongs.*

*Castle of **Haut Koenigsbourg***

*Castle of **Ortenbourg**. Completed in 1265 its remains are more impressive than its complex history : fought over for most of its existence, it was never lived in and is now owned by the city of Scherwiller.*

*left: A view of the town of **Kaysersberg** with the castle keep, one of the oldest in Alsace. The castle itself was pillaged by the peasants during the uprising of 1535, rebuilt, but still unable to withstand the onslaught of the Swedes who burnt it in 1632.*

It is a fallacy to think that castles were built only for military purposes. As well as being administrative centres, lieux de jurisprudence, castles generated a considerable income from the tolls that they levied when situated along trade routes and sources of water.

The social and economic growth of the cities in Alsace contributed to the decline of the castles in the 14th century as ten of them had been granted the status of free imperial cities, creating the *Décapole*. Power and wealth shifted from the mountains to the plains, as cities flourished and the nobility preferred the comforts of their urban residences to inaccessible and isolated citadels. Castles strategically located were modified and expanded to accommodate the advent of firearms, others were abandoned as they were too isolated and therefore too difficult and expensive to maintain.

Contrary to popular belief not all the castles were destroyed by the Swedes during the Thirty Years War, many were in fact razed to the ground by Louis XIV as he annexed Alsace to the rest of France.

*Castle of **Haut-Koenigsbourg**.*
The most beautifully and fully restored castle in Alsace. First mentioned in 1147 as belonging to Frederick Barbarossa. Strategically built at the crossroads of trade routes as a source of revenue, its high vantage point also made it virtually impregnable. In 1462 the castle was completely destroyed and its reconstruction began in 1479 thanks to the Swiss family Tierstein. Almost fully destroyed once again by the Swedes during the Thirty Years War, it was given to the Kaiser in 1899 who rebuilt it to look very much as it is today.
It owes its modern-day fame to Jean Renoir's film « La Grande Illusion » shot in 1936 with Jean Gabin, Erik von Stroheim and Pierre Fresnay, a monument of French cinema.

Castle of Landsberg. *Built over a long period of time, it is a significant landmark in the history of military castles in the area. It was expanded to accommodate the military needs of the conflicts between the Andlau family, close to the Emperor, and the Landsberg family, closer to the Bishop of Strasbourg. Due to the many power struggles, it changed owners frequently, and today is owned and maintained by the Baron Brice de Turckheim.*

Vosges du Nord

Castle of Spesburg. *Built of granite as a sumptuous residence for the solicitor, Alexandre de Dicka, of the Abbey of Andlau.*
Upon the death of the last heir in the Battle of Sempach in July 1386, it was ceded to the Counts of Andlau who subsequently left it to ruin.

Castle of New Windstein. *Built in 1339 to replace the castle of Old Windstein destroyed by the Bishop of Strasbourg six years earlier. The emphasis on comfort suggests that it was meant primarily as a castle to be used for residential purpose.*

$\mathcal{A}$LSACE

FROM SOUTH TO NORTH

The history of Alsace is rich and from the larger towns to the smaller villages, they all have a distinct history of their own. Colmar situated in the centre of the region and Mulhouse in the south are as significant to the Haut-Rhin or Upper Rhine as Strasbourg is to the Bas-Rhin or Lower Rhine, and reflect the different strands of the region's past.

***Dambach-la-Ville**, Bas-Rhin. A renowned wine growing centre surrounded by ramparts with three fortified tower gates enclosing superb 16th and 17th century houses. Once called Tannenbach or pineforest, fir trees figure on the town's coat of arms.*

MULHOUSE

The economic centre of the southern part of Alsace in the *département* of the Haut-Rhin, Mulhouse is considered the industrial capital of Alsace, and its second largest city. From a village of millers, it had become, by the 14th century, one of the ten free cities which formed the Decapolis, an alliance of Alsatian cities whose aim was to provide mutual assistance, particularly against rapacious nobles and bishops, and to resolve regional conflicts. However in order to preserve its independence, Mulhouse allied itself to the neighbouring Swiss cantons in 1515 and later adopted Protestanism as its official religion in contrast to the rest of the area which remained Catholic.

Place de la Réunion with City Hall – the City Hall was designed by a Swiss architect and erected in 1552. The outside decorations from the area of Lake Constance make it unique in France. A native of Mulhouse, Jean Gabriel added a new decoration in 1698. The shields bear the arms of the Swiss cantons and are a reminder of the links tying the city to its neighbouring country.

Société Industrielle. Founded in 1825 by 22 industrialists to promote industrial development, it also played a major role in the cultural and artistic life of the city.

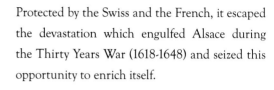

Musée de l'Impression sur Etoffe. Founded in 1955, the museum traces the history of printed fabric with thousands of samples. Demonstrations are given on the impressive machines. Printing and engraving techniques are explained to the visitor.

Protected by the Swiss and the French, it escaped the devastation which engulfed Alsace during the Thirty Years War (1618-1648) and seized this opportunity to enrich itself.

The earliest textile design workshop was created in 1746 and within a mere forty years, another 25 were established.

Promoting education, research and technical development, the city flourished remaining independent until 1798 when it joined the French Republic of its own accord for economic reasons.

The Industrial Revolution in the nineteenth century saw the rapid rise of its textile, automobile and chemical industries.

The Industrial Society of Mulhouse founded in 1828 made the city a precursor in terms of education as well as social projects for its workers with the creation of a mutual benefit society, the construction of the first workers' housing estates and the establishment of one of the first business schools in France.

The variety of unusual and interesting museums, in and around Mulhouse, which encompass fine arts, history, textiles, automobiles, railways, electricity, and even wallpaper attest to the impressive technological heritage of the area and make it well worth a visit.

left: **Riquewihr***, Haut-Rhin, Famous for its Riesling. Spared by the ravages of history, the town has retained the aspect it had in the 16th century. Nestled within the vineyards, it is one of the most colourful and typical villages along the Route des Vins.*

Kaysersberg*, Haut-Rhin.*
The first Tokay vines of Alsace were planted in the village and you can taste and buy excellent wines in some of the fine 16th century Renaissance houses. The birthplace of Dr Albert Schweitzer.

Close to Mulhouse lies the town of Thann, the southern-most point of Alsace's enchanting « *Route des Vins* » or Wine Road which winds itself northwards for 170 kilometres through the foothills of the Vosges to Marlenheim, passing through terraced vineyards and picture-postcard villages tempting visitors to linger.

Decorative and intricate wrought-iron street signs hanging from half-timbered houses with flower-bedecked balconies beckoning visitors to discover within, the gustatory charms of a winstub or restaurant. Vying for attention are the myriad of signposted invitations to a degustation or wine-tasting, offered by the local wine-growers.

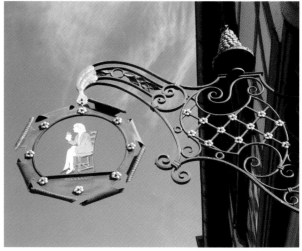

left: **Zellenberg**, *Haut-Rhin. The village is perched on a hill and offers breathtaking views of the wine growing countryside.*

left: A view of the village of **Rosenwiller**.

left: **Kientzheim**, *Haut-Rhin. The* **Château von Schwendi** *in Kientzheim is now fittingly the seat of the Confrérie de Saint-Etienne (the Brotherhood of St. Stephen) whose aim it is to promote and improve the quality of Alsatian wines. The château also houses a fascinating wine museum, Musée du Vignoble et Vin d'Alsace, dedicated to the art of winemaking.*

Hunawihr, *Haut-Rhin. The fortified church and cemetery surrounded by 14th walls and six bastions is still shared by Catholics and Protestants. A fountain dedicated to Saint Huna can be seen on the edge of the village. Legend has it that she washed the clothes of the indigent and the village fountain miraculously flowed with wine, after a poor harvest.*

*Typical 16th century houses in **Colmar**, Haut-Rhin.*

Petite Venise in Colmar. One of the most picturesque districts of Colmar, once inhabited by the market gardeners who would glide along the waterway in flat-bottomed boats to reach the market place

COLMAR

The attractive and picturesque town of Colmar considered to be the gate-way to the *Route des Vins* despite its half-way location is the seat of the *Conseil Interprofessionnel des Vins d'Alsace*, the Alsace Wine Committee whose aim it is to promote the *vins d'Alsace*, attribute the AOC label, and generally-speaking ensure the quality-control of the wines.

Its historic centre, quintessentially Alsatian, has been spared the rampages of the numerous armies of Austrians, Burgundians, Swedes, French and Germans which stormed through the region over the centuries. Miraculously, the historic centre was left intact while battles raged around the city at the end of the Second World War, devastating most of the neighbouring villages.

Blessed by a temperate climate, fertile soil and served by numerous waterways, Colmar was able to export its produce as far as the North Sea. Prosperous burghers built splendid Renaissance homes with ornate oriel windows and wonderfully carved facades.

A former Dominican convent, once the centre of Rhenish mysticism in the 14th century, the Musée d'Unterlinden is now the loveliest and one of the most visitied museums of France, housing artistic treasures from its heyday which include the remarkable Issenheim Altarpiece, a work of stunning realism and fantasy painted by Matthias Grünewald in the early 16th century. On display in the Eglise des Dominicains is the famous painting of the Virgin of the Rose Bower by Martin Schöngauer, a 15th century master engraver and painter from Colmar who influenced German art in the Renaissance period. Many of the fountains scattered around Colmar were donated to his home town by Auguste Bartholdi, the sculptor of the Statue of Liberty.

Ancienne Douane or Koifhus, Colmar. The main house dates from 1480. The ground floor of this former customs house was used to stock goods subject to municipal tax whereas the top floor was used as the meeting hall for the representatives of the Décapole, the union of ten Alsatian free imperial cities.

*Statue sculpted by **Bartholdi** in 1897 of Baron Lazarus von Schwendi who reputedly introduced the Tokay grape to Alsace when he returned from Hungary after fighting the Turks.*

BIBLIOTHÈQUE HUMANISTE
HUMANIST LIBRARY SÉLESTAT 67

Both a library and a museum, the *Bibliothèque Humaniste* in Sélestat has a rich and unique collection of over 3000 manuscripts dating from the 7th to the 16th century.

It is comprised of two collections, that of the Latin library founded in 1492 and belonging to the Latin School of Sélestat which formed many of the great men of the Reformation, and the private collection of the humanist, Beatus Rhenanus (1485-1547). His collection was unique in its time as the system of public libraries had not been set up and books were the province both of the elite and the Church. Upon his death, the renowned scholar and friend of Erasmus bequeathed his entire library of 670 volumes to his native city of Sélestat where it has remained since.

Other Renaissance libraries in Europe have been dispersed, but this collection remains an invaluable testimony to the intellectual ferment of the past. It includes such precious works as the 7th century Merovingian Lectionary, the oldest manuscript in Alsace, the 11th century Book of Miracles of St Foy and the *Cosmographiae Introductio* printed in 1507, the first manuscript to name America as the continent discovered by Christopher Columbus and later explored by Amerigo Vespucci.

Place de la Cathédrale, Strasbourg seen from the top of the cathedral

STRASBOURG

Strasbourg – a city where the present reflects the past. Stubbornly independent, it nurtured the great humanists of 16th century Europe who contributed to the social and religious changes which engulfed Europe during the Reformation. To this day Strasbourg continues to develop humanism by hosting a plethora of European institutions working in the aftermath of the Second World War to create and maintain a pluralistic, stable and democratic Europe.

Strasbourg has seen many peoples come and go in its long history, beginning with the Celts and then the Romans who established a military camp in 12 BC on an island on the river Ill surrounded by a bustling settlement of craftsmen and traders. Known as Argentoratum, it was at the crossroads of both the east-west and north-south trade routes. The Roman imprint can still be seen in the street plan of the old city around the cathedral. Destroyed by Attila the Hun in the 5th century AD, it was shortly included into the Kingdom of the Franks as *Stradeburg* or the city of the roads.

In 842, its strategic location made it the site of the Serment de Strasbourg or Strasbourg Oaths, the oldest official bilingual document written in both French and German which signalled the division of Charlemagne's empire by his grandsons. In 962, it was incorporated into the Holy Roman Empire, and in 1202, it obtained the privileges of "free Imperial City", dispensed from paying taxes to the Emperor and sending delegates to the Imperial Diet, a form of senate. Coins were minted in Strasbourg as early as the seventh century and were found throughout Europe, from the Baltic to the Black Sea. However it was not until 1296 that the city exercised its right to mint its own coin, which it continued to do until it was annexed to France by Louis XIV in the 17th century.

Bibliothèque du Séminaire. Library of the Collegium Wilhelmitanum built in 1722 as part of the Saint Thomas Chapter. It contains one of the largest collections of books and manuscripts from the 15th to the 20th centuries. The eastern wing, initially a convent, became a student's residence in 1544. The library was established to provide the students with research material and in 1894, when it celebrated its 350th anniversary, it already boasted 50 000 volumes.

Statue of the printer Gutenberg by the sculptor David d'Angers

*Reading Man in the **Parc de Pourtalès** on the outskirts of **Strasbourg**.*

The wealth of the city as well as its ecclesiastical importance was demonstrated by the construction of a magnificent cathedral. As a reflection of its mercantile character and independence, the city gradually evolved into a republic, establishing a constitution in 1334 and a governing council composed of noblemen, rich merchants as well as representatives from the various guilds. Strasbourg held its first trade fair in 1336, a tradition still present to this day. Indeed the *Foire Européenne* takes place yearly in September and welcomes thousands of exhibitors and visitors from around the world.

In the 15th century, Strasbourg obtained the right to give asylum to those banned or fleeing persecution from other European cities. Gutenberg thus found refuge in Strasbourg where he lived for approximately ten years and worked in secret on the printing press, his famous invention which was perfected and finalised in Mainz. In 1466, Jean Mentelin of Strasbourg used Gutenberg's revolutionary invention to print the first Bible in German. The printing press enabled humanist thinking to flourish in the following century also known as Strasbourg's *Siècle d'Or* or Golden Century when the city thrived economically and intellectually. Influenced by Erasmus, the city established educational institutions and fostered the publication of advanced medical and judicial texts. To this day, Strasbourg prides itself in having one of the best medical schools in France together with law faculties.

Religious reform was fervently preached by Geiler of Kaysersberg in the cathedral and by Martin Bucer, the minister of St. Thomas's. Tracts of Martin Luther's sermons were placarded on the cathedral doors, and in 1529 the city council banned Catholic masses and replaced them with Protestant services.

The 17th century was one of religious and military conflict resulting in much devastation with the "War between the Bishops": Protestant vs. Catholic, with the city supporting the Protestant postulate for archbishop, as well as with the Thirty Years' War when Strasbourg, supposedly neutral, sided once again with the Protestants. The Peace Treaty of Westphalia in 1648 ceded most of Alsace to the French, with the exception of Strasbourg. It was not until 1681 that the city capitulated to Louis XIV but the terms of its surrender stipulated that the city's basic religious, constitutional and economic freedom was to be respected.

Ponts Couverts

Strasbourg enjoyed a second *Siècle d'Or* during the 18th century. Although the cathedral was once more given over to Catholic mass, many churches were shared by Catholics and Protestants.

It became a city of refuge for Protestants persecuted elsewhere, and within the city, administrative positions were given alternately to representatives of each faith. The Jesuits as well as their Lutheran rivals expanded the university which attracted students from all over Europe including Goethe, the famous German poet.

Following the hardships and Puritanism of the previous century, there was an explosion of social and cultural activity, with theatres in French and German, and concerts by famous musicians, amongst them Mozart in 1778.

The end of the century saw political turmoil with the creation of a provincial assembly in 1787, and the ravages of the French revolution and terror. The newly-built *Hôtel de Ville*, city hall was ransacked and the cathedral's spire was covered by the red Phrygian bonnet, the symbol of the Revolution. Contrary to popular belief, the French national anthem, the Marseillaise, was actually composed in Strasbourg by Rouget de l'Isle, a young French army officer.

Ancienne Douane

Maison Kammerzell

Petite France

Aerial View

Parc de l'Orangerie

Petite France

European Parliament

Municipal Baths, Strasbourg. *Inaugurated in 1908, they are a splendid example of Art Nouveau architecture. Initially called the Russo – Irish Baths, they are the largest and most attractive baths still functioning to this day. Few homes had bathrooms and the primary function of the Roman Baths, as they are known today, was to provide the population with a place to wash.*

It is interesting to note that the baths also provided hydrotherapy for its clients: electrotherapy, mud baths, sulfur baths, a solarium and more… and even a bath for dogs. No longer in use today, they now serve as a municipal swimming pool.

In the 19th century Strasbourg saw the construction of the canals linking the Rhine to the Rhone and the Marne rivers, the advent of the railroad and the development of banking institutions.

The siege and bombardment of the city by the Germans during the Franco-Prussian war of 1870 resulted not only in many deaths and destruction, but also in Alsace being incorporated into the German empire. Befitting its new status as the regional capital of the Reichsland, the city was graced with grand boulevards and imposing buildings. A royal palace, the actual *Palais du Rhin*, as well as a new university, municipal baths, a library and a synagogue were built.

Strasbourg's population doubled and the city itself tripled in size with the construction of new neighbourhoods which included beautiful private villas for the wealthy in the Art Nouveau style.

Art Nouveau Building at 22, rue Sleidan, Strasbourg

In the aftermath of the First World War and the dissolution of the German Empire, Alsace once again became French. The hopes for more political freedom and economic prosperity were dashed as the situation deteriorated internationally as well as locally. In September 1939, on the eve of the Second World War, within two days the entire city was evacuated to the south-west of France, resulting in the German troops occupying a ghost city when they entered in 1940.

Evacuees who had decided to return to their homes, endured the subsequent «Germanification» of Alsace, leading either to deportation or forced conscription into the German army, a very painful episode in Alsatian history. Many of these *Malgré-Nous*, "Against Our Will", are still living with their painful memories to this day. The Allies bombed Strasbourg until the final stages of the war and in November 1944 the French flag definitively flew from the cathedral's spire.

Ponts Couverts, *remnants of the 14th century fortifications surrounding Strasbourg taken from the panoramic terrace of the Barrage Vauban built in the 18th century.*

*Summer terrace on the **Place Benjamin Zix***

The European Parliament

In the post-war years, under the guidance of forward-looking politicians, both local and European, Strasbourg began to reconstruct itself as the crossroads of Europe, becoming the seat of a number of institutions actively working towards European unity.

In 1949, the ten founding states of the Council of Europe chose Strasbourg to be its headquarters. This institution with 46 member states in 2004 seeks to promote and protect human rights, democracy and the rule of law. Its role is also to find solutions to social problems such as discrimination, xenophobia, AIDS, drugs, corruption, organised crime and terrorism. With the ratification of the « European Convention for the Protection of Human Rights and Fundamental Freedoms », the Council of Europe established an institutional system, the European Court of Human Rights, whereby individuals, in any of the member states, who feel that their rights are being violated, can complain to the Court against the state in question.

In 1979, Strasbourg was selected to be the site for the monthly and plenary sessions of the European Parliament, the parliamentary body of the European Union, an economic and political confederation of European countries, which in 2004 had 25 member states. The European Parliament is unique in that it is a supranational entity, whose members are directly elected by the citizens of its member states, and that it has legislative authority.

Among the various other European institutions located in Strasbourg are the European Science Foundation, the Institute for Human Rights, ARTE, the Franco-German cultural television channel and the Central Commission for the Navigation on the Rhine, noted for being the oldest European institution since it was established in 1856.

Strasbourg is the second hub of diplomatic activity in France due to the number of embassies, consulates and representations in the city. In addition, it boasts some of the best medical, science and humanities faculties in France together with research centres which attract students and lecturers from around the world. As a result, Strasbourg is an open and dynamic city with multicultural activities and a vibrancy to which the international presence strongly contributes.

Council of Europe

Human Rights Building

*A view from the heights of **Obersteinbach** in the Parc naturel régional des Vosges du Nord*

The *Vosges*

The Vosges Mountains

The Vosges mountain range stretches along the west side of the Rhine valley, running parallel to the river for about 200 kilometres, with fine forests of pine, beech, maple, spruce and oak. Luscious meadows provide green pasture for cows and sheep. The *Ballon d'Alsace*, rounded summits in the south of the region, offer picture postcard views of the Rhine Valley and the Black Forest, and on a very clear day, even the Alps are visible in the distance; the highest point being the *Grand Ballon* which culminates at 1424m. In summer, hikers and mountain bikers flee the heat of the plain for the cool forest trails which criss-cross the mountains. Superbly marked, these have been maintained by the *Club Vosgien* since 1872. In winter, skiiers and snow-shoe hikers escape from the fog blanketing the valley to the sunny slopes and ridges of the Vosges.

Transhumance - 'S WÀNDLE

Around the feast of Saint Urban on the 25th of May which signals the first day of summer according to the mountain calendar, herdsmen prepare their cows with the utmost of care and adorn them with highly decorative cowbells. They also don their traditional costumes prior to taking their herds up to the high pastures for the summer.

It is a festive occasion in the town of Wattwiller where locals and tourists join the herdsmen on their three-hour walk. A hearty meal and local festivities punctuate the event. On the feast of St Michael on the 29th of September, the cows are brought back down to the village where more celebrations take place.

The breed of cattle called *La Vosgienne* was imported to the area by the Swedes during the Thirty Years War in the 17th century. It is characterised by its hardiness and resistance to changes in temperature. The white streak along its back known as the *trace de lait* evokes the snow line along the mountain ridges.

The cowbells have a dual function: they help to keep track of the cows on the mountain slopes, but popular belief also has it that they ward off various mountain spirits.

The head cow, *die Meisterküeh*, wears the largest bell whose distinctive ring can be recognised by the herd. The leather straps are studded with brass tacks of various decorative motifs. The bell is engraved with the owner's name and the date it was cast. The craft of bell-making is an art form reflecting the life and aesthetics of the peasant community, and the oldest surviving bells date back to the early 19th century.

*Fête de la Transhumance in **Wattwiller***

North of the river Bruche, the Vosges are composed mainly of red sandstone, known as the *grès des Vosges*, used in the construction of castles, churches and imposing buildings throughout Alsace; the most famous being Strasbourg cathedral.

Also to be found are troglodyte houses carved into the rock, castles perched on outcrops of red sandstone as well as testimonials to more recent conflicts. Near the village of Lembach are the subterranean remnants of the Maginot Line, a defensive system built by the French between the two world wars.

The combination of an abundance of wood, water and sand also contributed to the development of glass-making in the region, crystal in particular; amongst the most renowned being Lalique at Wingen-sur-Moder whose factory still continues to produce beautiful crystal glasses, carafes and other decorative items.

The mountain village of **Steige**

Snow line on the mountain ridges of the **Route des Crêtes** *between the Hohneck and the Col de la Schlucht*

*Orchards with apple, mirabelle, cherry and quetsch trees in the **Obersteinbach** region*

The *Parc Naturel Régional des Vosges du Nord* has been designated a biosphere reserve by UNESCO.

South of the river Bruche, the red sandstone gives way to a granitic crystal-bearing and mineral rich rock structure. This, together with an ample supply of running water, led to the development of the mining and later the textile industries in towns such as Ste Marie-aux-Mines, the original home of the Amish who emigrated en masse to the United States in 1740.

The mountain pass above the *Val d'Argent* or Silver Valley, is the starting point for the *Route des Crêtes* built by the French during World War I to improve communication between the valleys along the front. This scenic drive which runs eighty kilometres along the ridge line of the Vosges, also known as *la ligne bleue des Vosges* for its distinctive blue horizon, passes through its most characteristic landscape of glacier lakes, high pastures above the tree line, and beautiful vistas over the mountains and valleys.

*Troglodyte homes, in **Graufthal** inhabited until 1958*

*Village of **La Petite Pierre***

*The « blue line » of the Vosges
from the **Hohwald** mountain*

*Fog in the meadows - Village of **Eschbourg***

The *Route des Crêtes* skirts the picturesque valley of Orbey, one of the oldest passages between Alsace and Lorraine where a French dialect called *La Welche* is still spoken. It winds its way past numerous *ferme-auberges*, working farms that double as inns where the typical dairyman's meal, the *Repas Marcaire* is served: a copious repast consisting of a *tourte* as starter, the local equivalent to a pork pie, then a *kassler* which is smoked pork shoulder accompanied by the unpronounceable *roïgabragedi* or simply sautéed potatoes, and served with a fresh green salad followed by farmhouse *Munster* cheese with a delicious, home-made fruit pie for dessert.

Mushrooming in the Vosges, a popular autumn activity in the region of **Niederbronn**

Autumn colours of **Grendelbruch***, larch trees*

*The Parc naturel régional des Vosges du Nord, région de **Graufthal***

Benfeld, « le Mort et le Traître »
Jewish cementary at *Oberbronn*
A view of le hameau des *Basses Huttes*, *near* *Orbey*
right: *Calvary,* *Calvaire near* *Marmoutier*

Jewish Heritage

The Jewish community in Alsace today is one of the most important after Paris, and this is in part due to the particularity of local laws which differ substantially from the rest of France. Alsace and the *département* of Moselle are the only areas in France to have retained an entire set of local laws known as the *Droit Local* which had been gradually implemented following the Franco-Prussian war when Alsace was annexed to Germany in 1870.

Despite Alsace having changed national identity several times since, it remains attached to the *Droit Local* which is a blend of French law prior to 1870, German law posterior to 1870 as well as additional laws. Religious equality is one area covered by these laws and the representatives of the different religions are treated as civil servants, and the buildings in which the services are held are funded and maintained by the French state or local authorities. In contrast to the rest of France, it is not uncommon to find Protestants and Catholics sharing a church, and the teaching of religion or ethics is still mandatory in primary schools. Alsatians traditionally retain a curiosity towards other faiths in a country where Catholicism is predominant.

The Jews of Alsace are believed to be the descendants of the Jews of Palestine who fled oppression in the 2nd century AD, and settled in Roman Gaul and the south of Germania. Documents attest to the presence of Jewish communities in towns and villages in Alsace in the 12th century when they took refuge from the persecutions of the second crusade in 1147.

Cemetery of Struth

Synagogue of Struth. *Built in 1836, it has been listed in the National Historical Monuments since 1987. The circumcision bench is also listed as it is an original built in 1886 and brought to the synagogue in 1995. All the elements of worship date back to 1850. The last service was held in 1969 and the synagogue became the property of the town in 1996. It is now fully restored to its original splendour after a five year restoration period and may be visited by appointment only.*

Synagogue of Bergheim. In 1349, the year the Great Plague broke out in Europe, nearly the entire Jewish community of Alsace was decimated, accused of having poisoned the wells. Whatever the community owned was confiscated, such as the Synagogue of Bergheim. Bought back by the Jews in 1551, it was restored several times and finally rebuilt in 1863. It is the only synagogue left in Alsace testifying to the presence of Jewish communities between the 14th and the 17th centuries.

Alsace was then part of the Holy Roman Empire and the Emperor took them under his protection: from being free men, they became the " property " of the Emperor, a double-edged sword since they were able to prosper but they had also become the target of reprisals.

They were initially craftsmen and merchants but with the development of the guilds, their crafts had disappeared as guild membership was restricted to Christians. They then turned to horse and cattle trading or peddling and as such they were often the only link between the villages. They were also money lenders, a profession prohibited to Christians, resulting in mounting tensions between the two communities.

As some 12th century documents from Strasbourg clearly show, Christians and Jews lived side by side in relative peace and prosperity to begin with. The outbreak of the Black Death in 1347 which lasted three years, killing 25 million people, dramatically changed the situation as the plague was frequently blamed on the Jews. Accused of poisoning wells and practising witchcraft they were either condemned to death or evicted, a ban enforced in Strasbourg for 200 years. The one hundred surviving families in Alsace fled to the rare villages which would accept them with quotas set of seven families per village. Judaism thus became rural, leaving behind a legacy of cemeteries and synagogues in villages throughout Alsace. The great reforms of the Humanist movement in the 16th century largely by-passed the Jewish population as they were forbidden to own land and were restricted to working either as money lenders, cattle or horse merchants, and even Protestant ministers such as Martin Luther continued to censor them severely.

The annexation in 1648 of Alsace to France brought about important changes and the lifting of certain restrictions. While the Jews suffered along with the rest of the population from the bloody conflicts of the Thirty Years War, they were the only ones who were willing to provide French soldiers with help and horses, since most Alsatians remained in their hearts attached to the German Empire and accepted the French under duress. Meanwhile the Jews saw this as an opportunity to find grace and protection from the French King: they were safe from aggression and reprisals as long as they served the King's interests.

As a result, Alsace experienced an influx of Jews from other parts of Europe fleeing persecution and seeking a better life. On the eve of the French Revolution the Jewish population of Alsace reached 20,000, nearly half of the entire Jewish population in France. The Jewish community was finally able to organise itself with rabbis holding religious as well as administrative functions, acting as the link between the communities and the royal authorities. In the middle of the 18th century, the rabbis were replaced by Jewish civil servants, the *préposés généraux* or general officers appointed by the *Intendant d'Alsace*, the governor of Alsace, to collect taxes and enforce laws. More than mere tax collectors, the *préposés généraux* were profoundly religious, wise men who wished to promote learning by building schools and synagogues, and contributed greatly to the economic and political development of the Jewish populace, culminating in their emancipation with the French Revolution in 1790.

Following the French Revolution and the closing of the borders, the Jews of Alsace once again found themselves living in rural isolation and in tightly-knit traditional communities. However their newly obtained civil rights finally gave them the right to engage in professions from which they were previously barred, acquire property and settle freely in cities. This progressive assimilation into French society drew them out of their economic misery, albeit at the price of a certain loss of identity. At the same time, they became fiercely patriotic with regard to the first country in Europe to have enfranchised them. In 1807 Napoleon created a structure for the Jews as he had for the Catholics and the Protestants with two consistories, one in the Bas-Rhin and one in the Haut-Rhin.

Synagogue of Ingwiller. The first temple was built in 1776 to serve one of the largest Jewish communities in Alsace. Another larger building was built in 1822 but the synagogue was not completed until 1891 with the addition of the women's gallery. The belltower dates from 1903. Having fled to the towns and villages during the Plague in 1348, the Jews seemed particularly welcome in Ingwiller where records show that market day was switched from Friday to Thursday to accomodate the Jewish merchants. As Ingwiller had been ceded by the Emperor to the Lord Simon de Lichtenberg, the town's Jews enjoyed peace and prosperity, and many of them even acquired the status of bourgeois. It is interesting to note that by 1850, 30% of the population was Jewish. They owned their homes and had a rabbi from 1833 to 1870. The population then decreased as Jews emigrated in order to avoid taking German nationality and serving in the German army.

Synagogue of Westhoffen
The new synagogue was built in 1860 to replace the older one of 1760 which had become too small. The oriental arches of the windows and the portal were probably meant to give it a distinguishing feature to contrast with neighbouring churches.

The Jewish community of Westhoffen was a fairly large one, particularly in the 18th century.

The relations between Jews and non-Jews seemed good: Christians would come and light the candles or warm the meals on Friday nights or Saturday mornings as Jews were respecting the rituals of the Sabbath.

In 1831, Louis-Philippe decreed that rabbis and officiating ministers would be paid by the State thereby giving them the same privileges as the other faiths. As a result, the Jewish population doubled once again and between 1840 and 1860, a large number of synagogues were either restored or rebuilt.

The defeat of the French army in 1870 was devastating for the Jews of Alsace who refused to serve in the German army. Many of them sold all they had and moved to other regions of France, North Africa or North America. At the same time, German Jews settled in the area and became wealthy industrialists. The French Jews who remained moved to the cities and the villages were progressively depleted of their Jewish population.

Alsatian Jews have suffered from anti-semitism to various degrees mainly due to economic circumstances, but no more than anywhere else. The Holocaust took its toll, wiping out one quarter of the Jews in the region. After the Second World War, those who survived came back to their communities to try to resume their life. In the 1960s the political situation in France provoked an influx of Sephardic Jews from North Africa making the Jewish population of Alsace one of the most important in the country.

Mikvé of Bischheim
A beautifully restored ritual bath with a 16th century staircase in Bischheim. In Jewish tradition, the mikve was more important than the synagogue itself because of the strict laws governing hygiene; it also served for women's monthly purification. The bath was dug out of the rock or the ground in order to capture the pure spring or ground water.

Cemetery of Rosenwiller. Records indicate that there was a Jewish cemetery in Rosenwiller as early as 1336. It was just a plot of arid land with small wooden boards to mark the site of the graves since gravestones were prohibited until the middle of the 18th century. While headstones were permitted after 1749, in 1793 the local administrator ordered their destruction. Few escaped the pillaging carried out by the villagers. An inventory of the graves is currently being carried out with special emphasis on finding more information on the rabbis and other known people as well as on the decorative motifs used on the stones. Although Rosenwiller did not have a synagogue, nearly 7000 people are thought to be buried in its cemetery.

What distinguishes Alsatian Jews is their uninterrupted presence in a much disputed region for over 800 years. Their history alternates between acceptance and rejection, tradition and modernity but for this people of wanderers Alsace has always represented the stability of a homeland. The numerous synagogues and cemeteries that remain in the villages to this day give evidence of a rich community life and an unshakable faith which allowed the Jewish people to live in peace with their neighbours and maintain the traditions that have kept them alive over the centuries.

Cemetery of Westhoffen

Cemetery of Weiterswiller. Between 1791 and 1870, the village counted 25 families, with a synagogue (now a private home) and a school. In 1808, by an Imperial decree of Napoleon, the Jews were imposed the choice of a family name which would then be passed down from generation to generation. Thus 105 people were officially registered at the town hall.

The **cemetery of Struth**. It dates back to the first Jewish inhabitants of the village in 1756. The oldest legible tombstone reads 1806. It is located on the outskirts of the village, built in two distinct parts on a slope, the oldest tombs being located in the upper part.

$\mathscr{F}$OLKLORE $\mathscr{E}$ $\mathscr{T}$RADITION

The stork is one of the most popular symbols of Alsace. It heralds the spring and is believed to bring good luck, good health and good fortune. Its legends are linked to ancient Germanic mythology: the souls of the dead were kept in an aquatic underworld and the stork's role was to place the soul into that of a newborn and deliver it to its parents. Thus, the stork symbolised the renewal and continuity of life.

A local legend, *La légende du Kindelesbrunnen*, has it that once upon a time, there was a lake under Strasbourg cathedral where the souls of the children to be would play and frolic while waiting to be reincarnated. A gnome in a silver-lined barque would delicately fish them out of the water and give them to the stork to deliver. For families desiring children, the tradition in Alsace was for women to put sugar on their window-sills to attract the stork. It is not uncommon to see stork nests perched on top of chimneys and church steeples. Thanks to the efforts of the *Centre de Réintroduction des Cigognes*, a centre for the reintroduction of the stork in Hunawihr along the *Route des Vins*, the stork population has risen from 9 couples in 1973 to more than 250 couples in 2001 and is still growing.

*Christmas **in the town-centre of Colmar***

CHRISTMAS IN ALSACE

Christmas in Alsace is a very festive season and one that every Alsatian looks forward to with anticipation. It is a particularly important religious celebration, perhaps more so than in any other region in France, and preparations start well in advance with the baking of cookies, the making of Advent calendars and Advent wreaths or *Adventskrantz*.

The wreath is an essential component of this holiday and has its place on every Alsatian table starting at the end of November. It is made of fir and mistletoe, and is graced with four red candles symbolising the four seasons and the four cardinal points, to be lit one at a time on each Sunday prior to Christmas. The wreath represents light, that is to say Jesus Christ, eternal life and the perpetual renewal of the cycle of life. In eastern Europe, the symbolism of the green crown is very strong: the association of light and vegetation is a sign of hope and revival after long and often harsh winters. With the lighting of the candles, families used to gather for afternoons of simple activities such as the confection of gifts or the reading of religious texts.

The Advent calendar is linked to this tradition as well. It usually represents the image of a village square with houses whose windows open in turn for each of the 24 days prior to Christmas revealing a verse from the Bible. In modern times, it has become a children's delight as the windows now no longer produce food for the soul but more earthly food in the form of a piece of chocolate!

Since the 12th century, Saint Nicholas has been a very important character in Alsace, and is also celebrated in nearby Lorraine, the north of France, Belgium, Germany, Holland, Switzerland and Austria. In Alsace, he is the patron saint of schoolchildren. It is believed that he was Nicholas of Myra born in the middle of the 3rd century AD. Many legends surround the saint, all of them emphasizing his kindness and generosity. Traditionally, he would go through villages dressed as a bishop to visit schools and distribute gifts and sweets to all the deserving children. He would also make his rounds going from door to door on the night of the 5th to the 6th of December with presents for the children who had behaved well. Those who had not, on the other hand, were exposed to the wrath of the *Père Fouettard*, or *Hans Trapp*, a sinister character all dressed in black with horns and a devil's tail or chains, whose mission it was to punish the naughty ones and generally speaking, frighten all the children in order to make the saint look a far more desirable option to strive for. The feast of Saint Nicholas is as popular and famous in Alsace as Christmas itself. There are many wonderful traditions at Christmas time which are not found in most other countries of the world.

One is the *Bûche* or Yule log. On Christmas night, the custom was to burn a log of oakwood and keep the remaining ashes and sawdust which had the power to protect the house from hail, lightning and fire or were strewn in the field to guarantee a good crop. The traditional Christmas dessert called the *Bûche de Noël* is served in every household and there are endless variations! While the emphasis is strongly on food in every good Alsatian home, the custom at Christmas is to fast before going to mass and break the fast afterwards in a warm and intimate family gathering.

A very special feature of Christmas time in Alsace is the *Christkindels-märik* or Christmas market which begins at the same time as the Advent calendar and which has been a tradition in Strasbourg for over 500 years. Although Christmas markets were seen mostly in the larger cities, the tradition has grown, and now many small towns and even some villages have one of their own. Small wooden huts crowd the town squares which are filled with light, and a joyous hustle and bustle. One can purchase local crafts as well as the traditional *pain d'épice* or gingerbread and the typical Alsatian *bredele* or Christmas cookies which come in all shapes and flavours.

Alsatian homes are filled with the wonderful smell of the *bredele* which are baked in large quantities throughout the entire month of December. Naturally, the *Glühwein* or mulled wine which one finds at the market is a must to heat the body and soul during that cold winter month. Christmas in Alsace is a celebration of light. Most villages are brightly illuminated as residents lovingly decorate the outside of their homes with many lights. Shop windows are brightly adorned, and the towns and cities throughout the region go to great lengths to create illuminated decorations that will bring joy to the streets. During the darkest time of the year light is everywhere, a symbol of hope, and a shield against sad and sombre thoughts.

RECIPES FOR *B*REDELE

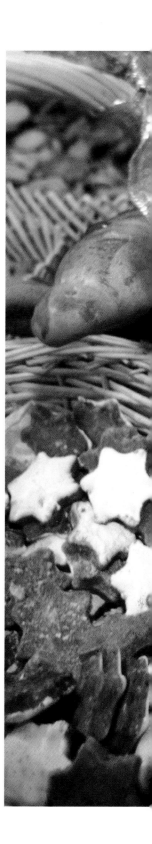

ANISBREDELE

550g (5 cups) flour
500g (2 and 2/3-cups) sugar
6 eggs
25g aniseed grains

Mix the sugar and the eggs. Beat for 20 minutes by hand or by machine. Add the aniseed grains, then the sifted flour.

Use 2 tsp of dough per cookie and place them on buttered and floured boards.

Let them dry overnight. Bake them the next day in a preheated oven at 150°C or 300°F. The top of the cookies should remain white.

SCHWOWEBREDELE

500g (4 ½- cup) flour
250g (1 and 1/3- cup) sugar
250g (9 oz) softened butter
150g (1 ½- cup) finely chopped candied orange and lemon rind
250g (2 cups) finely chopped almonds
grated rind of half a lemon
3 egg yolks
1 tbsp ground cinnamon
1/8 tsp ground cloves
1 beaten egg yolk

Sift the flour into a large bowl. Mix the butter with the sugar, the cinnamon, the candied rinds, the almonds, the grated lemon rind and the three egg yolks. Add the mixture to the flour and mix.

Let the dough sit overnight in the refrigerator.
The next day, roll out the dough and cut into various shapes, such as moons or stars.

Place the cookies onto a buttered cookie sheet and brush lightly with the beaten egg yolk. Bake in a preheated oven at 150°C or 300°F for 10 minutes.

ALSATIAN POTTERY

The tradition of pottery-making in Alsace dates as far back as the Middle Ages and continued to prosper until the middle of the 19th century. The first pieces were produced for domestic use: cooking and preservation pots were all made thanks to the abundance of clay in the area. It was a highly localised production as the pieces were too fragile to transport and as a result most towns and villages had their own pottery workshops. The technique of pottery-making became more refined as time went on and if the pots were porous and rather crude in their design to start with, their shape and purpose changed to acquire more sophistication as glazing was developed with the use of lead around the 13th century. In the 16th century a new technique was used called *Décor au Barrolet* which can still be found today, mostly on the pottery from the village of Soufflenheim. This technique involved an earthen pot with a small spout or goose feather attached to it, filled with coloured earth which was then used to decorate the pieces. Although the actual device has changed, this technique of decoration has remained. At the same time, modern types of earthenware crockery appeared such as plates, soup bowls, bowls with handles and the like. One could argue that this announced the beginnings of the *arts de la table* or the art of entertaining as we know it today.

Poterie Paul Schmitter, Betschdorf

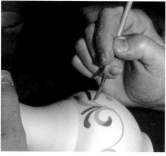

With the advent of industrialisation, the production of pottery as of many other man-made crafts declined after the second half of the 19th century and today, two important centres for pottery-making remain, those of Soufflenheim and Betschdorf. Even if potters tend to cater mainly to tourists these days, they have lost none of their charm and ancestral skills in that techniques have changed little and the pottery lover is certain to acquire a piece made with love and care. The grey and blue tones of the pottery of Betschdorf make it easily recognisable and distinguish it from that of Soufflenheim. It is made following a special technique imported from the Northern Rhine lands. The stoneware is baked at a temperature of 1250°C and sand is thrown into the fire to produce a beautiful translucent glaze. The grey tones are then decorated with cobalt blue. This technique has remained unchanged over the years but the potters are currently looking into using new colours to attract a clientele whose tastes and needs are more decorative than practical.

A superb 18th century farmhouse in the village of Betschdorf now houses the *Musée de la Poterie* or Pottery Museum where visitors can not only learn about the history of pottery-making in the area but can actually try their hand at making some as well.

POLYCHROME FURNITURE

© Pat Thiébaut

While painted furniture does not originate from Alsace, it has become part of the local tradition since the Middle Ages. The furniture is either fully painted in one colour, usually a deep red or imitation wood, or it is decorated with various motifs each with its own symbolism.

It was common to find that poor families would offer the bride or groom a decorated piece of furniture for their wedding. Their names and the date of their wedding would be painted on it and depending on the artist's verve, a touch of humour would be inserted as well.

Motifs varied from one area to the other, from rich floral decorations in the Kochersberg to geometric motifs in Alsace Bossue, or stylised roses, animals and figures in the south of Strasbourg. Techniques have evolved over the years but the most interesting is the symbolic meaning of colours and motifs.

Red was the colour of fire, blood, life and love and was widely used on wedding furniture. White symbolised light, birth and baptism. Blue was the colour of fidelity, a young girl portrayed with a blue ribbon meant that she was promised to a young man. Green meant nature, a non-festive period, the colour of hope and renewal. Violet was the colour of passion. Yellow had several meanings as it replaced the blinding colour of gold, the sun and God, but it also represented jealousy and hate. Brown and ochre were the colours of the earth, of humility and poverty.

The eye is immediately struck by the symmetry of the motifs.
The heart as the symbol of love is made of two commas in closed harmony.
The lozenge, the quadrilobe and the trilobe are symbols of creative forces, based on the union between man and woman.
Fruit, flowers and animals also carry a strong symbolic value: the presence of grapes is meant to bring abundance and wealth to the household. Snakes or loving turtledoves speak for themselves.
And lastly there is the horizontal eight, the symbol of eternity and that of mathematical numbers linking this motif to Christian numerology or various pagan beliefs.

ALSATIAN COSTUME

The way people were dressed determined the social category to which they pertained until the 19th century. Naturally poor peasants and wealthy city-dwellers did not mix and their dress clearly acted as social differentiation. This changed progressively after 1820. The French Revolution had taken place and people began to acquire a new sense of identity. At that time, one's style of dress rather than defining a person's social status became a reflection of his or her political inclinations or religious beliefs, age and even feelings.

The traditional costume that we see today was that of the peasants who expressed their very own aesthetic awareness. The various elements of the Alsatian costume were inspired by the style of the French nobility and bourgeoisie, and adapted to the local needs with variations from one area to the next. Women wore a white shift with ruffled cuffs and collars. A sleeveless tight-fitting bodice in dark velvet covered the shift made of lace or a plastron in the front. The skirt was long as befitted a modest, hardworking peasant woman with a full length apron. It was almost always red, a symbol of youth, health, wealth and love. Most noticeable was the head-dress which became increasingly elaborate over the years. Women usually wore their hair parted down the middle and the *coiffe* which started out as simple ribbons, gradually turned into something rather impressive which could extend outwards up to one metre!

Interestingly enough the colour of the head-dress or the ribbons adorning the bottom of the skirt revealed its owner's faith: Protestants tended to favour black whereas Catholics could be seen in less austere, brighter colours. The number of ribbons was a clear indication of their prosperity.

Men also had their traditional costume: black trousers with six gold buttons for bachelors, a white linen shirt, a red waistcoat and a black jacket. On their heads they wore a black braided broad-brimmed hat.

As a sign of the times the traditional Alsatian costume went out of fashion a long time ago and now belongs solely to folklore but the Alsatian people are highly attached to their traditions and will take advantage of any opportunity to bring out their local costumes.

© Pat Thiébaut

© Pat Thiébaut

ALSATIAN FOLKLORE ILLUSTRATED

The Alsatian way of life is traditionally portrayed in a particular type of folkloric illustration: men and women, boys and girls dressed in Alsatian costumes dancing in the village square, picking fruit, herding geese or strolling in the verdant countryside with an Alsatian village of half-timbered houses in the background.

These images are reproduced on china, silverware, tablecloths, teatowels, tins and other household ware throughout Alsace, bought not only by tourists but also by Alsatians themselves. Items depicting scenes of local folklore are as popular among its inhabitants as they are to the souvenir collector. Full sets of Alsatian-themed crockery known as the Obernai set by the local artist Henri Loux are on sale in the larger hypermarkets as well as in exclusive china shops and are found in most Alsatian homes.

The most ubiquitous and influential of Alsatian illustrators is Hansi, the pseudonym under which Jean-Jaques Waltz (1873-1951) is commonly known, an abbreviation of Hans (Jean) and I (Jacob).

A talented and prolific illustrator, lampoonist and writer from Colmar, he cultivated and defended Alsatian identity at a time when it had been undermined by the German Empire and once again during the Second World War. An ardent French patriot, he became a symbol of Alsatian resistance to German authority.

He is more famous today for his bucolic scenes of rosy-cheeked children in their colourful Alsatian folk costumes, but during his lifetime he engendered controversy for his political caricatures which also brought him fame. His legacy in both domains is still evident in Alsace as contemporary artists and caricaturists continue to be inspired by Alsatian folklore, tradition and a sense of identity.

© Pat Thiébaut

© Pat Thiébaut

Food and Drink

Alsace's reputation of a land of good food and drink spreads far and wide. Winstubs, once the property of the wine-growers, abound, serving traditional fare accompanied by fine wines. Bierstubs, formerly owned by the breweries serve foreign and local beers; the seasonal Christmas and March beers are always eagerly awaited.

Classic Alsatian recipes come from a long tradition of home-cooking made with local meats and seasonal produce. Endless and plentiful Sunday lunches provide the ideal occasion for warm family gatherings.

THE WINES OF ALSACE

The wines of Alsace are among the most famous wines in the world. By the Middle Ages, they were already praised as the best in Europe, reaching an apogee in the 16th century. The Thirty Years War in the middle of the 17th century devastated the vineyards and wine production all but ceased to exist. After World War I, it picked up again with an emphasis on quality which has been a priority ever since, with a strict geographical delimitation and a legislation governing production and vinification. As a result *Vin d'Alsace* has been an *Appelation d'Origine Contrôlée (AOC)* or official designation since 1962, *Alsace Grand Cru* since 1975 and *Crémant d'Alsace* since 1976.

In contrast to other wine regions in France, Alsatian wines are known by their varietal names: one does not buy a *Vin d'Alsace* but rather a Riesling, a Gewürtzraminer or a Sylvaner. This gives them a distinctive quality as each variety of grape has its own particularities. Ninety-one percent of Alsatian wines are white, all bottled in Alsace, and the characteristic flute-like shape bottle is protected by law.

The Vosges mountains create a natural barrier limiting the rainfall in the wine-growing region of middle Alsace. Blessed with a hot and dry climate in the summer, the wines mature slowly, and the different soils contribute to develop rich, complex and distinctive aromas.

When buying an Alsatian wine, one must therefore be attentive to the type of grape which must be mentioned on the label, only eight varieties of grapes qualify officially as *Vin d'Alsace.*

DIFFERENT WINES OF ALSACE

Gewürtzraminer, the spice *Gewürz* wine, is either loved or disliked but leaves no one indifferent. It is full-bodied, exuberant and seductive, and also qualifies as one of *Alsace's Grand Cru*. The Appellation *Grand Cru* is awarded on very strict criteria of quality, geographical location and a limited production. The label must mention the grape, the vintage and the exact origin of the wine. Gewürtzraminer goes well with strong cheeses such as Munster or blue cheeses as well as with *Foie Gras* and most desserts. It also complements spicy dishes.

Muscat is a wine which is also found in the South of France but the Alsatian variety is much drier. It is mentioned as far back as 1500 AD and also qualifies as one of the four *Grand Cru*. Muscat is an aromatic, lovely wine which goes well with asparagus, cold buffets, desserts or even on its own as an apéritif wine. In fact, one of the particularities of Alsatian wines is that they can all be enjoyed as an apéritif and don't necessarily need to accompany food as most other wines do.

Pinot Blanc is delicate, fresh and easy to enjoy. It is one of these wines which can be drunk with just about anything from roast fowl and seafood to light cheeses. It does not have a particularly distinctive aroma and is simply adaptable.

Pinot Noir is the only variety of grape to produce red wine in Alsace. Its light colour situates it between a red and a rosé, and when aged in oak barrels takes on a rich and complex aroma. Pinot Noir is the perfect wine for those who do not care for white wines, yet find red wines a little too heavy. Wonderful with most dishes, it is a true delight with powerful cheeses such as Brie, Camembert, Roquefort or other blue cheeses.

First mentioned in 1477, Riesling is probably the most well-known of Alsatian wines and another of the *Grand Cru* grapes. It is a dry, elegant wine with mineral or floral undercurrents which make it better when age slightly. It is best enjoyed with seafood such as oysters, shrimp or lobsters, but can also accompany roast fowl as in the famous *Coq au Riesling* and even goat cheese.

Sylvaner is light and fruity. It is a delightful thirst quencher which goes well with cold buffets and seafood.

Tokay Pinot Gris is a dessert wine. It is rich, even opulent with woodland undertones and a smoky aroma at times. The last of the four *Grand Cru* varieties, it has the reputation of a truly noble wine, alongside Gewürtzraminer.

*Maison Thierry-Martin
in Wangen, Bas -Rhin*

The four *Grand Cru* varieties can be used to make what is known in Alsace as *Vendanges* Tardives wines. The grapes are picked when they are over-ripe and the "noble rot" gives the wines their characteristically powerful aroma. *Grains Nobles* is the next step up. A higher sugar content produces a strong and complex wine which is so exceptional that it can only be enjoyed by an educated palate.

Last but certainly not least are the *Crémants d'Alsace*, sparkling wines made according to the traditional Champagne method. Pinot Blanc, Pinot Gris, Riesling and Chardonnay are used as well as Pinot Noir for a *Crémant Rosé*. Less costly than Champagne but serving the same purpose, the *Crémant d'Alsace* is fast becoming the leading sparkling wine in France.

Alsatian wines should be served chilled between 8° and 10°, and between 5° and 7° for the sparkling wines. The famous long stemmed glasses of Alsace are best suited for the wines as are the flutes for the *Crémant*. The bottles should be stored at a temperature of 10° to 15° in a horizontal position and should be left to mature anywhere from six months to five years.

*The **Caves des Hospices Civils de Strasbourg** dates back to 1395.*

ALSATIAN BEER

The origins of beer in Alsace can be traced back to the early Middle Ages when the Canons of the Chapter of Strasbourg were not only drinking it but making it as well, and this until the middle of the 13th century.

For almost 400 years, monks produced beer for the local population to replace water which was often undrinkable. The first "secular" brewery was founded in 1259 under the name Arnoldus of Strasbourg. Between the early 15th century and the middle of the 18th, beer-making developed considerably in the area to reach 34 breweries. Harsh winters and ravaging wars all but destroyed the wine crops and beer became a replacement for the wine shortage, considerably influenced by the presence of Nordic and Germanic populations.

Strasbourg was the main centre for beer-making and by 1870 the city counted 77 small scale traditional breweries with an additional 220 spread all over Alsace. The Industrial Revolution saw the invention of revolutionary techniques such as bottom fermentation, systems of refrigeration which enabled the brewing of beer at low temperatures, followed by Pasteur's discoveries on fermentation also known as pasteurisation which made for a healthier, germ- free beverage. The development of the railway system also contributed to bring about radical changes to the profession, transforming it into a real industry.

Alsatian beer began to be enjoyed in Paris in vast quantities by a new category of men, factory workers. Train loads of beer were sent to Lyon and the South of France, and at the *Exposition Universelle* of 1867, Alsatian beers were awarded numerous gold medals in recognition of their quality.

The larger breweries set themselves up in neighbouring Schiltigheim which became known as the *Cité des Brasseurs* brewers' town. The smaller breweries which could not afford to invest in such technological advances disappeared or were swallowed up by the larger ones such as Kronenbourg, Schutzenberger, Adelshoffen, and Fischer. Fairly important breweries were also located in Hochfelden, Saverne, Pfaffenhoffen, Mutzig and other towns in the north as well as Colmar, Lutterbach and Saint-Louis in the south.

One of the particularities of the beer industry in Alsace is that most of the drinking establishments were run by the breweries. As such, they were among the wealthiest real estate owners in the region. This also enabled them to have a much greater control of the distribution and sale of their production. The considerable wealth of the brewers who established themselves as a corporation and became the largest employers in the region gave them significant political power as well.

The beer industry was particularly dynamic and powerful, and contributed to the development of other related industries in the area. The end of the 19th century was truly a golden era. Today, seven breweries in Alsace produce 55% of the beer in France; Schutzenberger and Meteor are still family-owned while the others now belong to large industrial groups.

© Lola Thiébaut

Munster Cheese

Munster is derived from the latin Monasterium. The first mention of Munster cheese can be found in official documents dating back to 1371. It is widely believed however, that the cheese was already being made in Munster itself in the 8th century by the Benedictine monks who would save the milk and turn it into cheese to help feed the population. Later the cheese became part of the tithe that the peasants were forced to pay annually to the Munster convent or to the various feudal lords.

It acquired its official labelling in 1969, a guarantee of its origin and quality, and can only be produced in a specific geographical area. The cheese is also known as *Munster-Gérome*. It is still made according to traditional methods even though they have been modernised to comply with the latest rules of hygiene.

Once the cows have been milked in the evening, the milk is left to stand all night while a coat of cream forms on the surface. It is then incorporated to the morning milk and set to heat slowly in a copper cauldron. When the proper temperature is reached, rennet is put into the milk to make it curdle. The mixture sets for half an hour to allow the curd to separate from the whey. It is then retrieved, finely crushed and set in moulds to drip for two or three days. It is finally taken out of the moulds to be cleaned, salted and left to mature for a further three to four weeks.

The diameter of a Munster cheese varies from 13 to 19cm. Its texture is smooth, slightly humid and its colour ranges from light orange to red. Its potent smell is highly characteristic though its taste is surprisingly mild. While one would recommend a rich red wine with Munster cheese, it is best enjoyed with local wines such as Gewürztraminer, Pinot Noir or even beer.

Fromagerie Schuster at Orbey

EAUX-DE-VIE

Today, *eau-de-vie* or *Schnaps* is usually enjoyed after a good, hearty meal for its digestive properties. Its strong alcohol content of 45% and the rich, fruity flavours of mirabelles or yellow damsons, quetsches or wine-coloured plums or kirsch cherries make it a favourite in many a home and all the fine restaurants. It is a festive beverage often reserved for special occasions and sipped with parsimony.

This has not always been the case. *Eau-de-vie* has a most interesting sociological history. Behind the drink there were men, the *Bouilleurs de Cru*, independent distillers who turned *Schnaps* into a legend. It is important to understand the extent to which Schnaps was an integral part of Alsatian life and culture: it became a lifestyle.

It was produced exclusively in the *Schnapsgejed* the *Schnaps* region until the 1960s which included the foothills of the Vosgian mountains and their impenetrable villages in the valleys. It induced a characteristically archaic lifestyle that is to say a closed and conservative community, uneducated and superstitious, attached to its roots and traditions, not entirely hostile to new technology but distrustful, where drinking was rife. *Schnaps* distillers would drink half of their production to compensate for a diet which was poor in quantity and quality. Unlike today, *eau-de-vie* was a common beverage at the dinner table and at religious ceremonies. Because of the different varieties of fruit that were used, *Schnaps* punctuated the seasons of the year.

Strict laws governed the production and sale of *Schnaps*. It could only be distilled at specific hours and on certain days of the year, and its sale was highly taxed and strictly limited. The *bouilleurs de cru* had to have what was known as a *privilège* or the right to distil. They could distil their own fruit as well as the fruit the other villagers would bring. This *privilège* was transmitted from father to son but in 1960 a law came into force abolishing this right and only allowing it to be passed on to one's spouse. As a result, the *bouilleurs de cru* are an aging lot today and are slowly disappearing with the emergence of small-scale and industrial distilleries.

Schnaps has become a tourist attraction with *eau-de-vie* tasting as a regular feature on many guided tours. Alsace prides itself on having the best *eau-de-vie* in the world but it is more than just a drink; in Alsace, it is part of history.

Distellerie J.P. Metté
*at **Ribeauvillé***

Traditional Alsatian Delicacies & Recipes

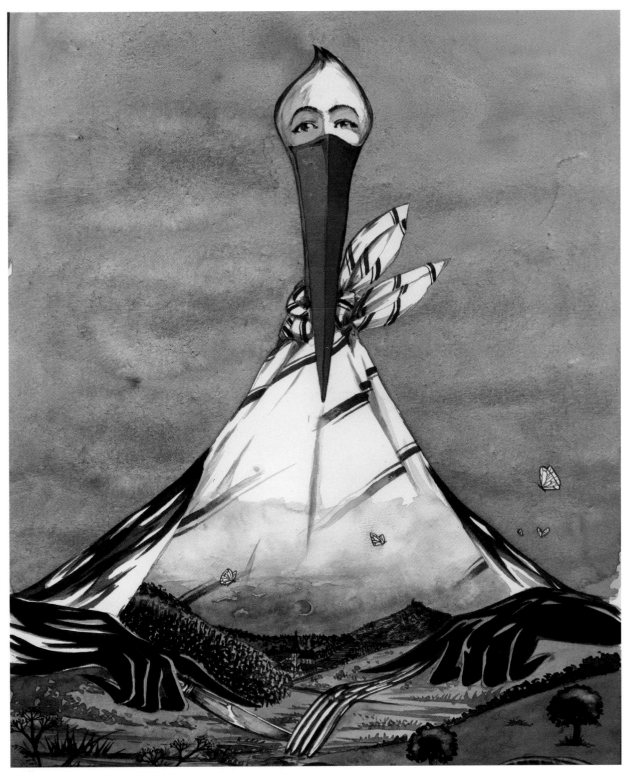

© Pat Thiébaut

Traditional Alsatian Delicacies

Recipe for Vinaigrette

Whip together :
5g (1 tsp) salt
a pinch of white pepper
1 tsp mustard
2 tbsp vinegar
4 tbsp vegetable oil

And add one hard-boiled egg cut into small pieces, one shallot or onion finely chopped, parsley and chives.

Coq au Riesling
The Alsatian variant of Coq au Vin usually served with Spaetzle

Asparagus
The first asparagus were planted in Alsace in 1873 by Pastor Heyler in the village of Hoerdt. Coming from Philippeville in Algeria where asparagus were cultivated, and struck by the poverty of the peasants in Alsace, he decided to try and grow asparagus in what was an inhospitable type of soil. Hoerdt has since become the asparagus capital and there is a small monument in front of the presbytery in honour of the man who saved the region from near famine.

Foie Gras
A gastronomic secret brought to Alsace by the Jews of central Europe, Foie gras is the fattened liver of a goose or duck once highly appreciated by the Romans. It is considered, along with truffles, to be one of France's greatest culinary delicacies. Its texture is rich and buttery and it is best enjoyed in Alsace with a sweet yet powerful wine, such as a Gewuertzraminer, a Tokay or better yet, a Vendanges Tardives. Traditionally served at Christmas and New Year in Alsace, it has been an essential part of the gastronomy since 1778 when a local chef by the name of Jean-Pierre Clauss invented a new recipe serving the Foie Gras cold in a crust known as "Pate de Foie Gras en Croute" for a rich Marquis.

Choucroute
The word comes from the Germanic term "surkrut" meaning sour cabbage. In other words, the cabbage is left to ferment for about three weeks prior to being used in the preparation of this Alsatian dish par excellence. Until WWII, it was common for families to prepare the cabbage themselves. It was also a very popular vegetable with the sailors: many of them were saved from scurvy thanks to its high vitamin C content.

Kougelhopf

It can be enjoyed as a dessert or as a savoury dish, made with bacon and walnuts to accompany a glass of wine as an aperitif. The most distinctive feature of this typical Alsatian "brioche" is the mould in which it is prepared. These earthen-ware moulds come from the villages of Betschdorf or Soufflenheim and are decorated in the distinctive local style.

Alsatian Cherry Pie

It is a delicious pie, a delight to both young and old. Given its fertile soil and temperate climate, fruit trees proliferate in Alsace, amongst them the cherry tree. The village of Westhoffen calls itself the Cherry Capital of Alsace and boasts 5000 cherry trees of different varieties.

Baeckeoffe

The word Baeckeoffe means baker's oven. This dish was traditionally served on a Sunday and only in the wealthier of homes as meat was a luxury. The lady of the house would prepare the dish on the Saturday and let it marinate until the Sunday morning when she would bring it to the baker for him to cook while the family was at mass. It would cook for about three hours but the entire process usually took 24 hours

Tarte Flambée

Flammekueche as it is known in Alsatian is the peasant's festive fare. They would bake their bread once every two or three weeks and to mark the occasion, they would spread the leftover dough on a wooden board, spread the base with soft white cheese and bacon, season with colza oil and bake in the oven. It would then be cut into pieces and in true Alsatian fashion eaten with one's fingers.

Traditional Alsatian Recipes

Tarte Flambée
Serves 6

Bread Dough
600g (5 cups) flour
1 packet dry yeast
2 tsp salt
1/4 litre (1 cup) water

Mix the ingredients and knead into a dough. Let it rise for 1 hour near a radiator or 2 hours at room temperature until doubled in size. Punch the dough down and divide it into 3 parts. Roll each part out into a rectangle on a floured wooden board.

Topping
1/2 litre (2 cups) creme fraiche or sour cream
100g (3 1/2-oz) finely chopped, sauted onions
100g (3 1/2-oz) lardons or diced streaky bacon
150g (3/4 cup) fromage frais or creamy cottage cheese
salt, pepper, ground nutmeg
1 tbsp of colza or another vegetable oil (optional)

Mix the sour cream with the cottage cheese and season accordingly with salt, pepper and nutmeg.
Spread the mixture onto the rolled-out dough and sprinkle the onions, then the diced streaky bacon on top. Lightly pour on the oil, if needed.
Bake in preheated oven at 250°C or 475°F for about 10 minutes.

Choucroute
Serves 6

1.5kg (3 lbs) sauerkraut
12 peeled whole potatoes
300g (2/3 lb) smoked pork blade
300g (2/3 lb) streaky bacon
500g (1 lb) salted pork belly
6 frankfurters
3 bratwurst
3 knackwurst
1 onion, studded with cloves
1 garlic clove
6 juniper berries
1 cup dry white wine
salt and pepper

Use a typical Baeckeoffe (earthenware) or a covered casserole dish.

Rinse the sauerkraut. Remove the rind from the streaky bacon and the smoked pork blade and spread the rind at the bottom of the dish.
Add the sauerkraut, the onion, the garlic, the juniper berries and the white wine. Salt and pepper lightly.
Add the smoked pork blade, the salted pork belly and the streaky bacon, and bake in a preheated oven at 210°C or 410°F for one and a half hours. After 45 minutes of cooking, add the potatoes and 30 minutes later add the sausages.

This recipe can also be prepared in a heavy stovetop casserole dish on a burner.

Baeckeoffe
Serves 6

750g (1 1/2- lb) juicy beef, cut into cubes
750g (1 1/2- lb) juicy pork, cut into cubes
half a pig's trotter
1 kg (2 lbs) peeled, finely sliced potatoes
300g (2/3 lb) finely chopped leeks
300g (2/3 lb) finely chopped celery root
500 g (1 lb) finely chopped onions
3/4 litre (3 cups) dry white wine
vegetable oil
salt, pepper, thyme, bay leaves, nutmeg, cloves to taste

In a typical Baeckeoffe dish, start with the pig's trotter, then layer the vegetables and the meat. Repeat this process twice, ending with a layer of potatoes. Add salt and pepper, and season to taste.
Pour in the wine until it reaches 3/4 of the casserole dish. Add a touch of oil and cover. Marinate overnight.
On the following day bake in a preheated oven at 200°C or 405°F for at least 3 hours.
Serve with a green salad

Coq au Riesling
Serves 6

Kougelhopf

Alsatian Cherry Pie

Pie Crust
300g (2 1/2- cups) flour
50g (1/4- cup) sugar
125g (4 1/2- oz) softened butter
1/8 tsp baking powder
1/8 tsp salt
1 egg yolk
water (optional)

Filling
Cherries or other seasonal fruit such as
mirabelles or yellow damsons, quetsches or
plums, or apples.
1 beaten egg
30g (1/8 cup) sugar
1 cup of milk or light cream

Sift the flour with the baking powder and
make a well. Beat the butter with the
sugar, the salt and the egg and add the
mixture to the flour. Work the dough and
add some water if too dry. Let it stand for
at least an hour, if not overnight.
Roll out the base and place it in a buttered
pie dish.
Prepare the custard by mixing the egg
together with the sugar and the milk or
cream.
Fill the base with the fruit and bake for
10 minutes in a preheated oven at 210°C or
410°F.
Pour the custard over the fruit and bake
for another 30 minutes.

500g (4 1/2- cups) flour
150g (6 oz) butter
120g (2/3 cup) sugar
2 eggs
1/4- litre (1 cup) milk
1 packet dry yeast
50g (1/3- cup) raisins
25g (1/4- cup) chopped almonds or
walnuts
1/2- tsp salt
a shotglass of Kirsch
powdered or icing sugar

Soak the raisins in warm water
until soft. Warm the milk, add the
sugar and the butter. Sift the
flour, make a well, add the yeast
and the eggs. Mix with some of the
surrounding flour. Add the milk and
the salt, mix with the rest of the
flour, and finally add the raisins and
the kirsch.

Knead the dough by hand for
15 minutes (the dough should not
stick). Let it rise for 1 hour in a
warm room. Butter the mould,
sprinkle the almonds or the walnuts
at the bottom, put in the risen
dough and let it rise a second time
to the edge of the mould.

Bake in a preheated oven at 210°C
or 410°F for 50 minutes. Wait
5 minutes before removing from
mould, let it cool and sprinkle it with
powdered or icing sugar.

One chicken thigh per person
150g (5,5 oz) button mushrooms
3 shallots or 1 big onion, finely chopped
12cl (1/2 cup) heavy cream
50g (2 oz) butter
1 tbsp oil salt, pepper
5cl (1/5 cup) Cognac
30cl (1 1/4 cup) Riesling

Heat the butter and the oil in the saucepan.
Place the chicken thighs skin-side down and allow
to cook on a low heat for 5 minutes. Salt and
pepper lightly. Add the shallots or the onion
and heat until tender; then pour the Cognac
over the mix and light. Add the mushrooms
and the Riesling, cover and simmer for 30 to
40 minutes. Withdraw the chicken parts, add
the cream and reduce the liquid. If the sauce
is not thick enough, add 2 tbsp of flour and a
little extra heavy cream.

Spaetzle
500g (2 1/2 cups) flour
5 eggs
50g (2 oz) butter, 10g (1 tbsp) salt
125 ml (1/2 cup) water

Sift the flour in a large bowl. Beat the eggs
with the salt and the water and add to the
flour. Beat the mixture energetically with
a wooden spoon until it bubbles. On a lightly
floured board, roll the dough out as flat as
possible and cut into thin strips. Toss the
strips into boiling salted water. The spaetzle
are ready once they have risen to the surface.
Strain them out and rinse under cold water.
This can be done ahead of time.
Before serving, saute in butter.

INDEX

© Pat Thiébaut

ℬIBLIOGRAPHY

Alsace: Hachette Vacances, Hachette UK, London, 2002.

Alsace, Lorraine, Champagne: The Green Guide, Michelin, Watford, 2001.

James Bentley, Alsace, Penguin Books, London, 1990.

Jean-Louis Delpal, ed., Alsace: Guide Minerva, Editions Minerva, Geneva, 1995

Encyclopédie de l'Alsace, Editions Publitotal, Strasbourg. 1982.

Georges Foessel, Jean-Pierre Klein and Roland Recht, Connaître Strasbourg, Editions Alsatia, 1988.

Georges Livet and Francis Rapp, ed., Histoire de Strasbourg, Editions Privat/DNA. 1987.

Parc Naturel Régional des Ballons des Vosges: Guides Gallimard, Editions Nouveaux-Loisirs, 1999.

Marie-Christine Périllon, Strasbourg The European, Editions Hoëbeke, 2003.

Tom Stevenson, The Wines of Alsace, Faber and Faber, London, 1993.

Strasbourg, Editions Bonneton, 1993.

Jean-Claude Streicher and Jean-Charles Pinheira, L'Alsace, Editions Ouest-France, Rennes 1995

Sue Style, Alsace Gastronomique, Conran-Octopus, London, 1996.

WE ARE GRATEFUL TO THE FOLLOWING COMPANIES FOR SUPPORTING US IN THIS PROJECT.